Body Talk

Defend Yourself

THE IMMUNE SYSTEM

Steve Parker

Raintree

Chicago, Illinois

For information, address the publisher
Raintree, 100 N. LaSalle, Suite 1200
Chicago, IL 60602
Customer Service   888-363-4266
Visit our website at www.raintreelibrary.com

Printed and bound in China, by South China Printing
Company Ltd

10 09 08 07 06
10 9 8 7 6 5 4 3 2 1

Library of Congress Cataloging-in-Publication Data
Parker, Steve.
    Defend yourself! : the immune system / Steve Parker.
        p. cm. -- (Body talk)
    Includes index.
    ISBN 1-4109-1880-7 (library binding - hard cover) --
ISBN 1-4109-1887-4 (pbk.)
    1. Immune system--Juvenile literature. I. Title. II. Series:
Parker, Steve. Body talk.
QR181.8.P37 2006
616.07'9--dc22
                                                2005027516

Acknowledgments
The publishers would like to thank the following for
permission to reproduce photographs:
Alamy Images pp. 36-37 (AGStockUSA, Inc./David Reede),
pp. 26-27 (Sally and Richard Greenhill), p. 9 (Shout);
Corbis pp. 8, 14, 17, 19, 21, 24-25, 40, 42; 40-41 (Al
Fuchs/ NewSport), pp. 20-21 (Bettmann), p. 33 (Cameron),
p. 13 (Layne Kennedy), p. 7 (Sygma/ Kent Tony); Creatas
pp. 10-11; Getty Images p. 20 (Brand X Pictures), pp. 38-
39 (PhotoDisc), pp. 42-p. 43 (Stone), p. 35 (Stone/Alan
Thornton); Harcourt Education Ltd/Tudor Photography p.
29; PhotoDisc/ PhotoLink pp. 4-5; Science Photo Library p.
37 (AJ Photo), p. 36 (Andrew Syred), pp. 14-15 (Astrid &
Hanns-Freider Michler), p. 16 (BSIP VEM), p. 38 (Edwige),
pp. 34-35 (BSIP, Laurent), p. 30 (Custom Medical Stock
Photo), pp. 32-33 (David Goodsell), pp. 6-7 (David Scharf),
pp. 12, 22 (Dr P. Marazzi), pp. 30-31 (Dr. John
Brackenbury), p. 24, (Ed Reschke Peter Arnold, Inc.), pp.
12-13, 22-23 (Eye of Science), pp. 8-9 (J C Revy), p. 18 (J.
L. Carson, Custom Medical Stock, Photo), pp. 18-19
(Lauren Shear), pp. 16-17 (Prof. P. Motta/ Dept. Of
Anatomy/ University "La Sapeinza", Rome), p. 25 (R.
Umesh Chandran, TDR, WHO), p. 31 (Simon Fraser/ Dep't
Of Haematology, RVI, Newcastle), pp. 28-29 (St
Bartholomew's Hospital), p. 15 (Steve Gschmeissner).
Cover photograph of people in protective clothing
reproduced with permission of Getty Images/Stone/Stuart
McClymont.
Artwork by Darren Lingard and Jeff Edwards.

Every effort has been made to contact copyright holders of
any material reproduced in this book. Any omissions will
be rectified in subsequent printings if notice is given to the
publishers.

The paper used to print this book comes from sustainable
resources.

Disclaimer
All the Internet addresses (URLs) given in this book were
valid at the time of going to press. However, due to the
dynamic nature of the Internet, some addresses may have
changed, or sites may have ceased to exist since publication.
While the author and publishers regret any inconvenience
this may cause readers, no responsibility for any such
changes can be accepted by either the author or the
publishers.

Dedicated to the memory of Lucy Owen

Contents

Any words appearing in the text in bold, **like this,** are explained in the glossary.
You can also look out for them in "Body language" at the bottom of each page.

3

Always On Guard!

Have you and your body ever had one of those days? In the morning you wake up, get out of bed, and stub your toe on the door frame. Later in the morning you scrape your finger and it bleeds a little.

In the afternoon the chain comes off your bike, and your hands get covered with greasy dirt that is hard to wash off. In the evening you start to feel slightly hot with a runny nose, as if a cold is coming.

Feeling OK again

And yet, a couple of days later, you're fine! Your bruised toe and scraped skin heal, your hands are clean again, and the cold never came. Your body has coped with the problems, mended the damage, and defended itself against germs.

Self-defense

The human body protects itself all the time. There are always germs around, tiny and unseen. Dust and dirt are everywhere too. The body regularly rubs and bumps itself in small ways, and occasionally suffers a bigger bruise, scrape, or cut. But most of the time, the body deals with the problems. It has many kinds of self-defenses to keep out germs, kill them if they get in, combat disease, and repair injuries and damage. As you eat, walk, talk with friends, go to school, watch television, and sleep, your body is always on guard.

◄ Some activities are more dangerous than others. But the body has amazing powers of self-defense and healing, although it sometimes needs medical help.

Find out later

What kind of eggs could be in dirty food?

Why are some bacteria friendly?

Why can't we stop getting colds?

First Line of Defense

When people like firefighters go into dangerous places, they wear protective clothing. But in a way, all our bodies have protective clothing. This clothing covers us almost all over, resists many kinds of harm, and even repairs itself. It cannot repel serious dangers like fire, but for day-to-day use it does a good job. This protective clothing is our skin.

Tough covering

Your skin has two layers that help defend you. The layer you can see on the outside is the **epidermis.** It is thin but tough, elastic yet strong. What's more, germs or scrapes cannot kill it, because it is already dead.

Even better protection

Skin makes natural oils and waxes, called **sebum.** These coat its surface and keep it flexible and elastic. Sebum is also part of the body's defenses. It keeps out water and contains natural substances that help to damage or kill germs.

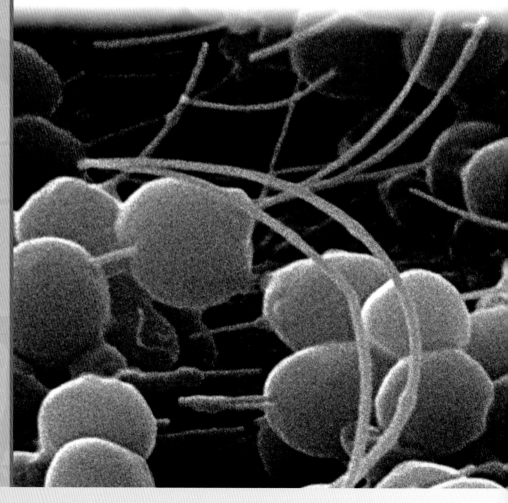

cells   microscopic building blocks that make up all body parts
epidermis   outer layer of skin, constantly renewed from underneath

Replace

Like all body parts, the epidermis is made of micro-sized building blocks called **cells.** Your whole body is made of billions and billions of cells. Most of them are very much alive and busy. But the cells of your skin's outer layer are hard, tough, and dead, and they are soon worn away. They lock together like tiles on a roof or bricks in a wall, to keep out dirt and germs. As they are rubbed off, they are replaced by more dead cells, millions every hour.

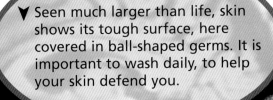

▼ Seen much larger than life, skin shows its tough surface, here covered in ball-shaped germs. It is important to wash daily, to help your skin defend you.

Hairy cover

Tiny hairs cover most of the body, giving added defense to skin. Longer, thicker hairs on the head also protect us from a bump or the sun's fierce rays. However, the length of these hairs is up to us, depending on our haircuts and lifestyles.

New coat every month

Every four weeks, you look like a new person. The outer layer of skin you had last month is not the same as the layer you have today. Tiny pieces of skin gradually flake and fall off your body all the time as you move around, wear clothes, wash or shower, and towel dry afterward. As the pieces fall off, they carry with them dirt and germs. This is part of the body's defenses.

New for old

If skin is always flaking away from the body, why don't we end up red and raw? Because the rubbed-off pieces are always being replaced by new skin from underneath. At the base of the **epidermis, cells** divide quickly to make more cells. The new cells gradually move up to the surface, pushed

Thick-skinned

Skin is thickest on the soles of the feet, where it gets pressed and rubbed most. Any area of skin that gets regular use responds by growing thicker, for good protection. Thickened patches of skin are called **calluses.**

▲ At the base of the skin's outer layer, millions of microscopic cells multiply every second.

calluses   patches of thick, hardened skin
keratin   tough protein that makes skin resistant to wear

by cells below. At first they are shaped like hamburger buns, but after a couple of weeks they are more like pizzas. As they are forced up, they flatten out even more and become bent, like warped cafeteria food trays.

Nonstop replacement

The whole journey for these skin cells may be just a millimeter or two. All the way through, they fill with the tough body substance called **keratin.** By the time they reach the surface, they are flat, dead and ready to be worn away.

Extra help

Sometimes skin gets more than its usual wear very quickly. This can happen in just a few minutes. Then it cannot cope and may get rubbed raw or swell up as blisters. Extra defenses like gloves (above) can stop this from happening.

BUCKETS OF SKIN

Every second the body loses about 50,000 tiny flakes of skin. Over a lifetime that adds up to about 88 pounds (40 kilograms).

Where we feel touch

Our sense of touch comes from the lower layer of skin, the **dermis.** This has millions of tiny sensors to detect light touch, heavy pressure, heat, cold, movement, and pain.

Get away!

When a pesky fly lands on your skin, you brush it away or swat it. And when danger is near, like cars on the road or the flames of a fire, you are alert and ready to move. This is also a way that your body defends itself. This defense is not your body's physical structure. The defense is your actions and movements.

Touch and feel

Your sense of touch is especially important for this kind of protection. If you detect something unusual on your skin, you want to find out what it is and whether it is harmful.

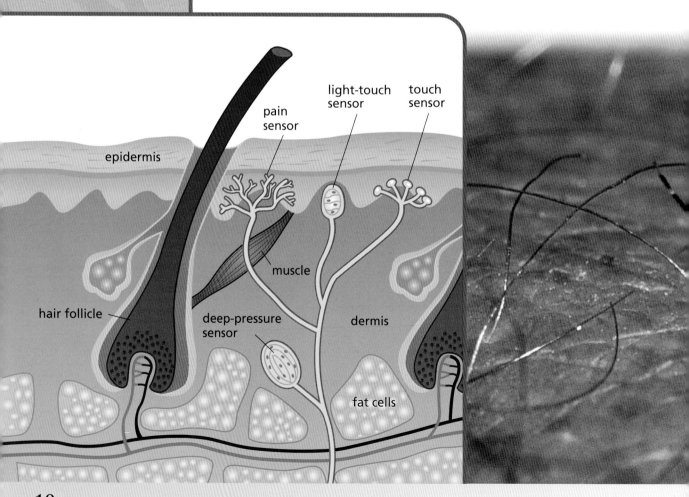

light-touch sensor

touch sensor

pain sensor

epidermis

muscle

hair follicle

deep-pressure sensor

dermis

fat cells

dermis   inner layer of skin containing sweat glands, hair roots, and nerve sensors

Your sense of touch can often tell if it is hard or soft, sharp or blunt, hot or cold, rough or smooth. This helps you decide whether everything is fine, or whether you need to defend yourself by taking action and perhaps moving away.

Damage limitation

If your skin does suffer harm, like a cut, bite, or sting, it warns you by feeling painful. Then your behavior continues to protect your body. You act to limit the damage. You wash and clean the area and maybe put on a bandage. You are careful not to bump the area so that it heals fast. In this way your actions and behavior help your body defend itself.

Automatic defense

Sometimes our brains are too busy to notice a sudden danger. So the body has its own built-in defense actions, called **reflexes.** They are fast and automatic, happening before we even realize it, like pulling the hand away if it touches a hot plate.

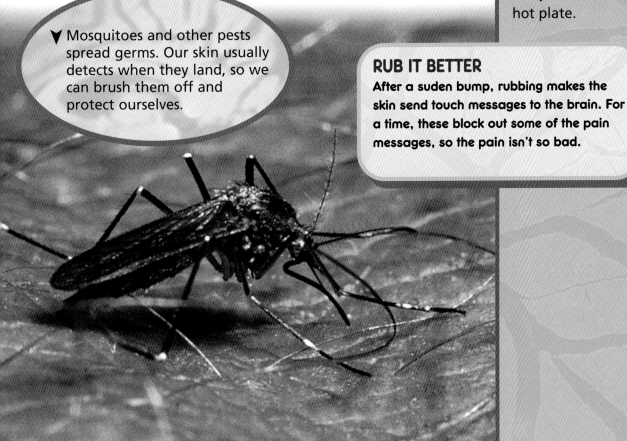

▼ Mosquitoes and other pests spread germs. Our skin usually detects when they land, so we can brush them off and protect ourselves.

RUB IT BETTER
After a suden bump, rubbing makes the skin send touch messages to the brain. For a time, these block out some of the pain messages, so the pain isn't so bad.

Just a scratch

Where did you last cut or scratch yourself? Did it bleed much? One of your body's best defenders is your blood. Usually it flows around and around inside its **blood vessels.** But if your skin gets cut or broken, then blood oozes out of the wound.

A fast seal

Blood defends you by **clotting,** or turning into a sticky lump at the wound. It seals the wound to stop blood from flowing out and prevent germs and dirt from getting in. Usually enough clotting to stop the bleeding takes only a few minutes. You can help by cleaning the cut as soon as possible and putting on a bandage. This gives added defense against dirt and germs and also prevents the clot from being scraped off.

▼Under the microscope, a clot appears as a tangle of tiny fibers, sticky substances, and millions of platelets.

Medical help

A big wound may bleed so fast that the blood cannot clot. So the doctor or nurse puts in stitches (above) or clips. These hold the wound closed so blood can do its defense work.

clot lump of blood that seals a wound
blood vessels arteries, capillaries, and veins through which blood flows

Clump and clot

Clotting involves about a dozen natural chemicals in blood. It starts with **microscopic** pieces of cells called **platelets**. Activated by an **enzyme,** the platelets flow to the wound and form a plug. A net of protein threads forms and traps the platelet plug. Gradually the net spreads and gets thicker. Over a day or two the clot hardens into a scab that protects the skin beneath while it heals. The scab eventually falls off.

HEMOPHILIA

In the condition called hemophilia, which is inherited (passed on in families), blood lacks certain clotting chemicals. Without these, blood keeps oozing from a wound. Hemophilia can be treated by injections of the missing chemicals.

Plant blood

Plants like pine trees have a defensive fluid called resin. When the tree suffers a cut, sticky resin leaks out and gradually becomes hard or clots. Over millions of years, lumps of resin become hard yellow amber. Sometimes this contains insects that got trapped in it when it was soft and sticky.

Under Invasion!

There are dangers all around you, but they are far too small to see. Germs drift through the air, float in water, and land on objects and surfaces, even though they look clean. Everything has germs on it, including your body. The body must constantly defend itself against them.

The good and the bad,

Not all bacteria are harmful germs. Many are harmless and live in the soil. Some are even friendly and live inside our own bodies, helping us take in nourishment from food. Bacteria in yogurt helps our bodies digest food.

Types of germs

What are the main types of germs? One group is **bacteria.** The cells of your body are very tiny. Bacteria are even more **microscopic.** About 100,000 would fit into this o. Different bacteria cause problems like sore throats and skin boils as well as serious illnesses like TB (tuberculosis).

Another group of germs is the **viruses.** These are many times smaller than bacteria.

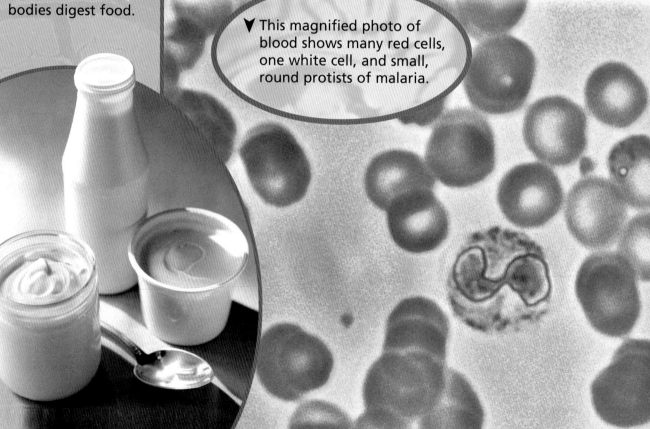

▼ This magnified photo of blood shows many red cells, one white cell, and small, round protists of malaria.

bacteria   microscopic organisms of many types
protists   one-celled organisms

About one million viruses would fit into the dot in this i. Viruses cause illnesses like colds, flu (influenza), and measles. A third group of germs are **protists.** These are about as big as the body's own cells and different kinds cause different diseases, such as **malaria.**

Getting in

Skin is good at keeping out germs. But they are always trying to get into the body through skin cuts and wounds, by being breathed into the nose, windpipe and lungs, or swallowed in food or drinks. However, the body has defenses for all these entrances.

and the ugly.

All kinds of viruses are harmful. They multiply by getting inside the body's own cells and destroying them. Most viruses are also very tough. They can survive after being dried out, frozen, or even boiled.

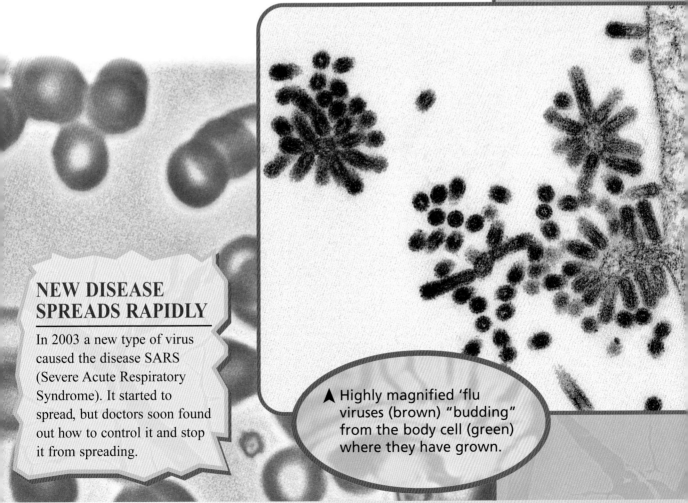

NEW DISEASE SPREADS RAPIDLY

In 2003 a new type of virus caused the disease SARS (Severe Acute Respiratory Syndrome). It started to spread, but doctors soon found out how to control it and stop it from spreading.

▲ Highly magnified 'flu viruses (brown) "budding" from the body cell (green) where they have grown.

The acid bath

When you eat food and swallow drinks, they go down into your stomach and immediately get attacked. Inside the stomach are very powerful juices, called **enzymes,** and natural acid. Their main task is to **digest** lumps of food into smaller and smaller pieces, to pass through the body.

Chemical defense

The **digestive juices** and acid have another function. They help kill germs that come in with the foods and drinks. The acid attacks each germ's outer covering. This makes the germ unable to multiply, and it can even kill it. This is one of the body's methods of chemical defense.

Worms as germs

Sometimes harmful worms inside the body cause serious illness. They get in as tiny eggs on unclean food, in dirty water, or perhaps on dirty hands or eating utensils.

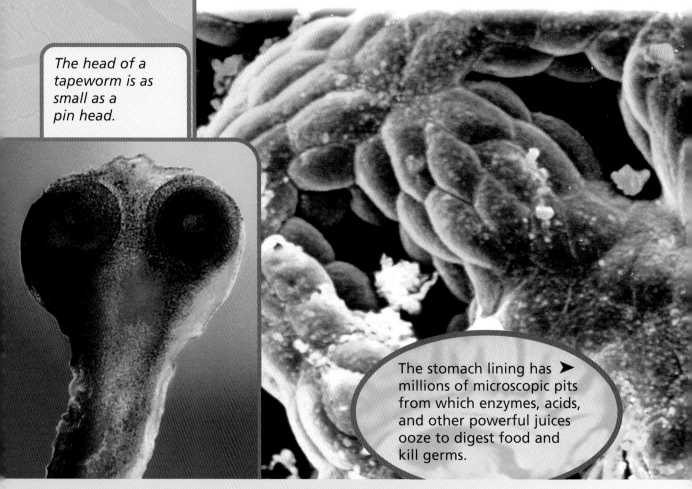

The head of a tapeworm is as small as a pin head.

The stomach lining has ➤ millions of microscopic pits from which enzymes, acids, and other powerful juices ooze to digest food and kill germs.

Body language

digest   break down food into smaller and smaller pieces
digestive juices   liquids in the digestive system that break food apart

Too many to kill

The stomach's acid and juices can cope with most types of everyday germs. But sometimes unusual germs get in, perhaps by the millions. This can happen if we drink unclean water, or eat old, bad food, or food that has not been cooked properly. In these cases, enough germs survive in the stomach to multiply. They then cause a type of illness known as food poisoning. Germs that do this include salmonella and listeria.

Help your stomach

You can help your stomach defend you in various ways. Avoid foods that look moldy or bad, or that smell strange. Check your foods' expiration dates. Wash hands well before preparing, cooking, and eating food, especially if using your fingers!

---

enzyme substance that controls the speed of a chemical change, such as occurs during digestion

When nose is best

The nose has small hairs at its entrance to catch floating dust. And it has its own type of sticky mucus to trap germs and other tiny particles. This double defense cleans the air before it gets to the lungs.

Ready and waiting

Special rooms in hospitals and some factories have incredibly clean air, filtered to remove all dust and germs. But for most people, every time we breathe germs from our environment float into the nose, down the throat and windpipe, and into the lungs. The respiratory system's defenses are ready and waiting.

Sticky trap

The insides of the nose, the windpipe, and the lung airways are designed to trap dust and germs. Their inner linings continually make the slimy substance **mucus**. Dust and germs get stuck in this mucus and cannot escape. The linings also have millions of microhairs called **cilia**. These move like tiny boat oars to push the mucus along. It flows like a very slow, sticky river, up the air tubes and windpipe and into the throat. We cough it up and swallow it as **phlegm** when we clear our throat.

mucus

cilia

◄ The sticky mucus and cilia microhairs work nonstop to clean dust and germs from the body's air tubes.

cancer disease caused when body cells multiply out of control and spread, causing growths or lumps called malignant tumors

Not just germs

The respiratory system doesn't only protect against common germs. It also traps tiny floating airborne toxins, like those in the exhaust fumes of cars and trucks. If these tiny particles are collected in the lungs, they could cause very serious diseases such as **cancer.**

COUGH, SNEEZE

Sometimes a sticky blob of mucus or too much dust gets trapped in the nose. We sneeze to blast air through the nose and blow out the blockage. If the same thing happens in the windpipe or lower airways, a cough does the same job.

Extra defense

When there are many small particles or droplets floating in air, the body's breathing system may need more protection. A face mask helps to filter out the problem particles. This is very important when working with powders, sprayers, grinders, and sanders.

cilia   microscopic hairlike projections on the cells of various body parts

Battle in the Body

When did you last have an infection? What exactly is an infection? Every day, some germs manage to get through your body's outer defenses through a tiny cut in your skin or when you breathe or swallow.

Once inside, the germs have warmth, moisture, and nourishment, especially if they are in the blood. They try to multiply and spread through the body. An illness caused by germs is an infectious disease or infection. If the germs are spread by very close contact (mainly touch), the infection is said to be **contagious**.

In-between time

The time between coming in contact with germs and feeling ill is called the **incubation period.** It varies from a day or two for some germs to months with others. The person may still be able to pass on the germs to others during the incubation period.

The chickenpox incubation period is 12-21 days. It then causes itchy spots.

▼ In this 1918 influenza (flu) epidemic, hospital wards overflowed. Some hospitals tried curing patients with fresh air.

contagious   spread by close contact
lymph   pale fluid that flows through vessels and ducts and transports white blood cells

Inner defenses

If germs get into the body every day, why aren't we always ill? Because the body not only has outer defenses, it has a whole range of inner defenses. They involve many body parts, especially the blood and another body fluid called **lymph,** as well as structures called **lymph nodes** or glands.

Stopping the spread

People with dangerous infections such as ebola (above) will be cared for in hospital isolation rooms. This stops the germs from spreading to other patients. The medical staff wear masks, caps, and gowns to protect themselves.

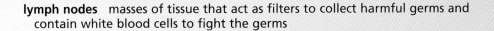

lymph nodes masses of tissue that act as filters to collect harmful germs and contain white blood cells to fight the germs

21

First response

When germs invade or damage occurs, the body starts a process called **inflammation.** White blood cells gather and fluid collects at the site of damage or invasion, so that the main defenses can begin. This makes the part swollen, tender, and hot, but usually the imflammation fades as the defenses win.

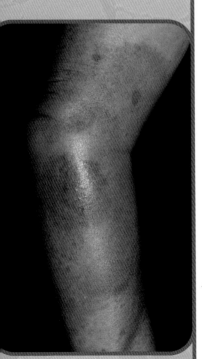

Microdefenders

Some of your body's best defenders are blobs of pale jelly so small that 1,000 could fit into this o. Millions of them patrol day and night, on the lookout for germs and other unwanted substances. These champion defenders are called **white blood cells.**

Not well named

The name white blood cells is not quite true. They are not white, they are colorless. And not all of them live in the blood. Like tiny plastic bags full of clear jelly, they can change shape to squeeze out of the blood vessels. Then they push between other body cells, hunting for germs. Since there are blood vessels all over the body, white blood cells can reach every body part.

White blood cells can push ➤ out long, fingerlike projections to move and to search for germs.

macrophage

macrophage   white blood cell that eats bacteria and other unwanted germs

Big eaters

There are several kinds of white blood cells involved in body defenses. One kind is the **macrophage** (below). This name means big eater. A macrophage oozes along, searching for germs. When it finds one, it flows around it and engulfs it, taking it inside. Within the macrophage, powerful **enzymes** attack the germ and destroy it.

More defenders

When germs infect the body and multiply, white blood cells mutliply too, as part of the defense system. Their numbers can increase tenfold in two days. This helps the body to resist the invaders.

E.coli bacteria

AMAZING FACTS

In one drop of blood the size of a pin-head, there are about 5,000 white blood cells.

Some kinds of white blood cells, like macrophages, live just a few hours and eat more than 100 germs each.

Other kinds of white blood cells survive for many months.

white blood cells colorless cells in the blood that fight germs and disease

Coming and going

Lymph does not flow around and around like blood. It starts as watery liquid from inside and around cells, that oozes into the tiny open ends of lymph vessels. The vessels join into larger **ducts.** The two biggest ducts join to blood vessels in the chest, where lymph merges with blood.

Defense highways

Most cities do not rely on one transportation system. They have roads, railways, perhaps an underground subway, and maybe even waterways. The body has different transport systems, too. These allow its **white blood cells** and other defenses to move around quickly and get straight to the site of trouble. The main two transport systems are blood and **lymph.**

Blood

Blood flows around and around the body in a branching network of **blood vessels,** pumped by the heart. During an infection, white blood cells in the blood search and destroy germs there. The white cells can also move out of the tiniest blood vessels, the **capillaries,** to fight any germs among other body cells.

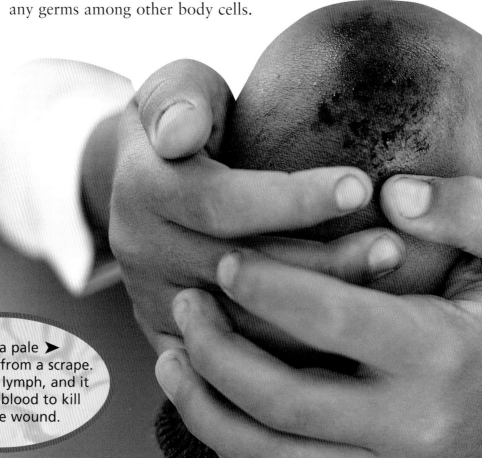

Sometimes a pale ➤ fluid oozes from a scrape. This fluid is lymph, and it works with blood to kill germs in the wound.

ducts   pipes or tubes for liquid
parasitic   living with, in, or on an organism, causing harm to the organism

Lymph

Sometimes when you have a small cut or scrape, no blood comes out. This means you have not damaged a blood vessel. Instead there may be clear or pale fluid, called lymph. Like blood, lymph flows through the body carrying millions of white blood cells. But it moves much more slowly because it has no pump of its own. It is pressed and squeezed through its tubes, called lymph vessels, by the muscles around them as the body moves around.

Too much lymph

Rarely, tiny **parasitic** filarial worms get into the lymph system and block its flow. Lymph fluid collects and causes huge swellings. The result is filarial disease, also called elephantiasis.

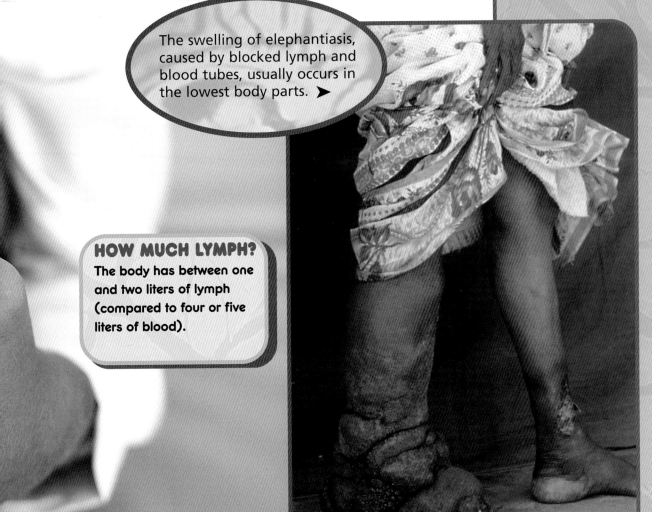

The swelling of elephantiasis, caused by blocked lymph and blood tubes, usually occurs in the lowest body parts. ➤

HOW MUCH LYMPH?

The body has between one and two liters of lymph (compared to four or five liters of blood).

Lymphatic system

The lymphatic system consists of lymph fluid, lymph vessels and larger tubes called ducts, and lymph nodes.

Centers for defense

When people are ill, their glands may swell and ache. They form painful lumps under the skin, often in the neck or armpits. These glands are actually **lymph nodes,** and they are part of the lymphatic system. There are also lymph nodes in the chest, the lower body or abdomen, and the groin. They also swell during illness, but we cannot feel them because they are deeper within the body. The smallest lymph nodes are the size of rice grains, while larger ones are as big as grapes. But in a serious illness, they can swell as big as tennis balls.

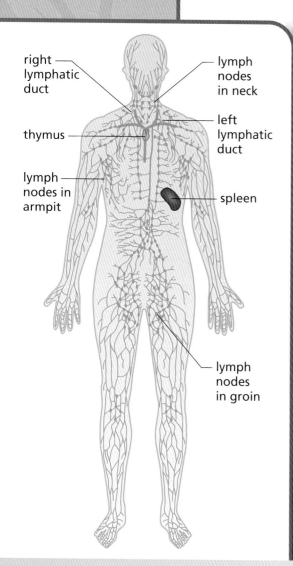

right lymphatic duct

lymph nodes in neck

thymus

left lymphatic duct

lymph nodes in armpit

spleen

lymph nodes in groin

Swollen glands are really ➤ enlarged lymph nodes, a sign that the body is battling against germs.

Packed with defenders

The lymphatic system's main job is to defend the body by resisting infections and other illnesses. Lymph nodes are centers for this defense. They are packed with many kinds of white blood cells. Some of these multiply rapidly to make more white blood cells. The white cells travel through the lymph and blood and ooze out between the body cells to combat germs and disease.

Inside a defense center

Lymph fluid flows into a node through several tubes, but out from only one. Inside the lymph node, white blood cells multiply and then spread around the body to attack germs.

White blood cells multiply in the lymph node's germinal centers.

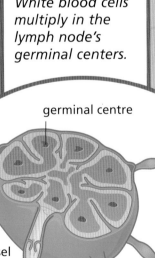

germinal centre

outer capsule

lymph vessel from node

lymph vessel to node

Guarding the entrance

Most parts of the lymphatic defense system are hidden inside the body. But two structures are much nearer the outside. These are the **tonsils** and the **adenoids.** The tonsils are two masses of tissue in the throat. They contain many kinds of **white blood cells.** The reason for their location is because they are helping guard against germs that get into the body through the mouth. The tonsils are well placed to defend against germs in foods and drinks.

Helping to clean air

There are similar masses of tissue called adenoids behind the nose. The adenoids are very active in young children. They help defend against germs inhaled while breathing in air and to kill germs trapped by **mucus** in the nose. Normally, the adenoids shrink and often disappear by the early teens.

Body gatekeepers

The tonsils are on either side of the upper throat, on the lower edges of the tongue's base. The adenoids are at the lower back of the nasal chamber (the space inside the nose).

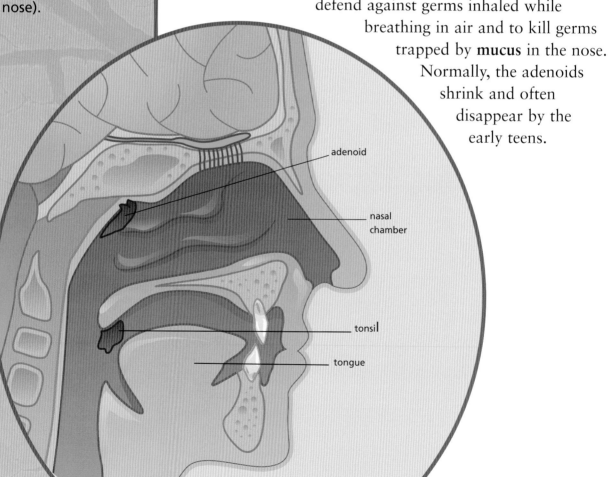

adenoid

nasal chamber

tonsil

tongue

adenoidectomy operation to remove adenoids
tonsillectomy operation to remove tonsils

Too big

In some younger people, tonsils or adenoids become overactive. They remain swollen for much of the time. Enlarged tonsils cause a sore throat and painful swallowing. Enlarged adenoids make the voice sound odd, and block the nose so the person has to breathe through the mouth.

Treatment

Sometimes swollen tonsils and adenoids are part of a general illness. But if they stay too big for too long, they can be removed by an operation. This is a **tonsillectomy** or **adenoidectomy.**

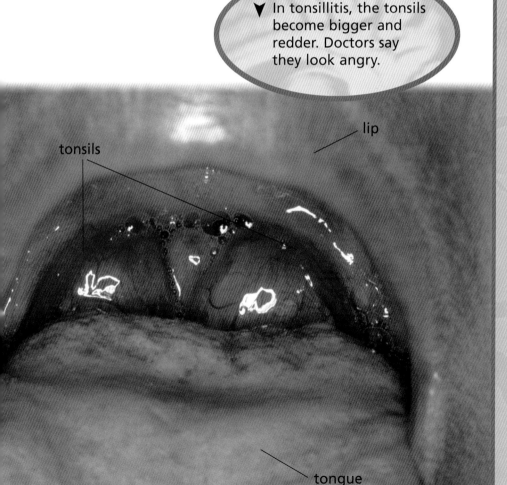

▼ In tonsillitis, the tonsils become bigger and redder. Doctors say they look angry.

tonsils

lip

tongue

Your Ever-Ready Army

Training camp

The **thymus** is a gland just behind the breastbone, shaped like two sausages side by side. It is part of the **lymphatic** system, as the main "training site" for the white blood cells called lymphocytes. This is where the lymphocytes multiply and gain their germ-fighting powers. Trained lymphocytes are called T-cells (T for thymus).

Have you ever visited an old fort with its massive walls and tall guard towers? Well defended places like fortresses have many lines of defense. Your body is the same. If germs get past the outer defenses, and even the first inner defenses, the body has an army inside to fight them.

The defense deep inside is the **immune system.** It involves various groups of **white blood cells** and other cells, as well as various natural chemicals. All these move around the body in the blood and lymph to wherever they are needed. The immune system also acts against illnesses that are not caused by germs from outside, but which start inside the body, like some forms of **cancer.**

donor   person who gives something
immune system   cells and body structures that protect the body from illness

Chief defenders

The main defenders in the immune system are the white blood cells called **lymphocytes**. Like other white blood cells they can change shape and move anywhere. Millions die each day in the battle against germs and disease, and the body makes millions more. They are produced in the jellylike marrow inside bones. **Bone marrow** makes other kinds of white blood cells, too, as well as **red blood cells** that carry oxygen around the body.

▼ If you don't manage to get out of the way of someone sneezing, the germs will find their way inside you. That's why you need your immune system.

Bone marrow transplant

In some people the immune system's lymphocytes do not work properly. One treatment is bone marrow **transplant.** Marrow from another person, the **donor,** is injected into the bones. This healthy marrow should then make fully working lymphocytes.

DESPERATELY SEEKING A DONOR

In a bone marrow transplant (right), the bone marrow must be specially selected as exactly the right type or match for the patient. Otherwise the patient's immune system will try to fight the new blood cells and lose even more strength.

lymphocytes   type of white blood cells that fight germs
thymus   gland near the heart that is part of the lymphatic system

The protection squad

How do white blood cells like **lymphocytes** recognize germs from among all the body cells? And once recognized, how do lymphocytes destroy the germs?

Identification card

All body cells carry special molecules on their surfaces that communicate with the **T-cells.** These molecules hold substances called **antigens.** Some antigens come from **bacteria, viruses,** and **toxins.** T-cells can tell these apart from the body's normal cells.

Lots of antibodies

During an average healthy person's life, the body produces millions and millions of antibodies. For someone who is ill often, the number could be even higher.

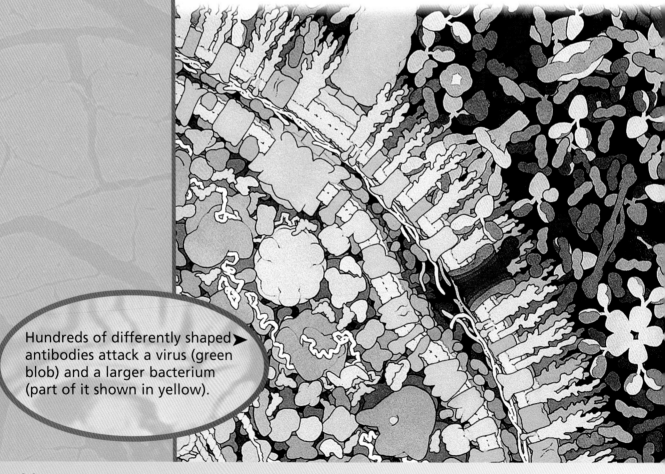

Hundreds of differently shaped ➤ antibodies attack a virus (green blob) and a larger bacterium (part of it shown in yellow).

antibodies substances made by the immune system that attack antigens

The T-cells can also recognize the exact type of antigen. These lymphocytes then instruct other types of lymphocytes, the B-cells, to make one of the immune system's main weapons, **antibodies.**

Germ warfare

Antibodies are body chemicals designed to fight germs. They float in the blood and **lymph.** Each kind of antibody is specially shaped to fit onto the antigen of a particular type of germ. When the antibody attaches, it makes the germ

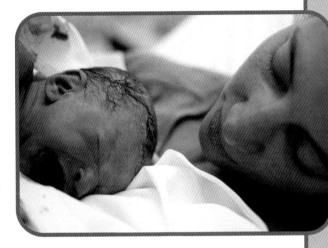

harmless, or stops it from multiplying if it is a virus. During an infection, this happens every second to thousands or millions of germs all over the body.

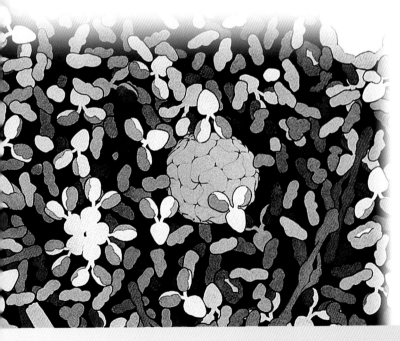

Ready-made 1

A new baby takes in antibodies from its mother both in the womb and after it's born, when it drinks her milk. These ready-made antibodies protect the baby against certain diseases for a while, until its own immune system develops and becomes stronger.

Ready-made 2

People traveling to places where certain diseases are common may get an injection to stay healthy. It contains ready-made antibodies against the germs for those diseases. This is not the same as the body making its own antibodies.

antigens substances that are not part of the body and are recognized and attacked by the immune system's antibodies

Routine types of vaccines, and the age they are given at, vary around the world. Some of the common ones are:

MMR – Measles, Mumps, and Rubella (german measles)

DTaP – Diphtheria, Tetanus, Pertussis (whooping cough)

Polio – Poliomyelitis (given by mouth, not injection)

BCG – Against TB (tuberculosis)

Influenza (or flu)

Hepatitis

Tricking the defenses

Can you remember having some injections when you were young? You may have had one recently too. These injections protect you against certain serious, even deadly diseases. What is in these injections and how do they work?

Long memories

After a germ infects you, some of your **lymphocytes** become memory cells. They remember how to make the **antibodies** that fight the germ. If the same germs get into your body later, the immune system can make massive amounts of the correct antibody quickly. The germs are destroyed before they can multiply and cause disease. This is known as becoming **resistant** or **immune** to that infection.

Fooling the system

To protect you against germs that you might come across in the future, your immune system can be tricked into making the special antibodies that you will need. You have probably had a **vaccination** before. The **vaccine** contains dead or disabled versions of the germs. Or it may contain harmless versions of the **toxins** made by the germs. Your immune system thinks it's under attack and responds as usual by making antibodies.

The first time around, building defenses to new germs takes time. If you pick up germs the normal way, they multiply and make you ill before you can develop any immunity. But the modified germs in the vaccine cannot cause the illness, so there is no disease. Your immune system is only working to build up its weapons.

The immune system is now ready to combat the germs much more quickly, if you pick up the germs again. The whole process of becoming resistant is called **immunization.**

Changing germs

Vaccines do not work against some diseases, such as the common cold. The viruses that cause colds are always changing their **antigens.** The body becomes resistant to one version, but does not recognize the next, and so on. So we cannot develop an immunity, and continue to get colds most years.

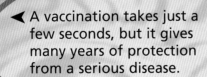

◄ A vaccination takes just a few seconds, but it gives many years of protection from a serious disease.

vaccine substance containing modified versions of a germ, which prepares the immune system to defend against the real germs

35

Asthma

In some people **asthma** attacks can be triggered by a tiny creature, the dust mite (below). It lives in house dust and, like all animals, produces droppings. These dry out and float as powder. In the lungs, an allergic reaction to the droppings makes the airways tighten up, making breathing wheezy and difficult.

Harmless yet harmful

Do you know someone who gets **asthma** or **hay fever?** Maybe you get them yourself. These conditions are called **allergies.** They are caused by the system which is supposed to protect the body, the **immune system.** Allergies happen when the immune system goes for some reason into overdrive.

Mistaken identity

The immune system is supposed to defend the body against germs and harmful substances. An allergy is a case of mistaken identity.

If you are allergic, your immune system attacks substances that do not bother other people at all. In hay fever, the harmless substance is the tiny **pollen** grains of plants like grasses, trees, and flowers.

allergic reaction   processes such as inflammation or coughing as the body fights a substance that is harmless to most people

These float in the air like specks of dust too small to see, mainly in spring and summer, and we all breathe them in.

Overreacting!

Inside the nose of a person with hay fever, the immune system goes into action as if the pollen grains were germs. The nose swells inside and becomes runny, itchy, and sneezy. The same may happen when pollen touches the eyes, making the eyes runny, red, and itchy. This is your immune system overreacting and trying to get rid of the pollen.

◀ Pollen from grasses and crops like wheat is spread by the wind and also by machines like combine harvesters.

FOOD ALLERGIES

Certain foods cause allergic reactions in some people, including peanuts, shellfish, and strawberries.

The reaction can make the face swell and the skin develop a red rash. The airways can even close up and this can kill.

People with severe food allergies should carry medicines all the time in case they accidentally eat one of the dangerous foods.

Treatments

There are several kinds of inhalers for allergic conditions like hay fever and asthma. They deliver medical drugs directly to the site of the problem—inside the nose for hay fever and deep into the lungs for asthma.

asthma condition, often linked to allergy, where the bronchioles get narrow and fill with mucus, making breathing difficult

No immunity

Some babies are born with an immune system that does not work. The cause is often unknown. With no defense against germs, the baby must stay in special germ-free surroundings (like the one below). One hope of treatment is a **bone marrow transplant.**

Defenses down

One of the newest and most serious diseases around the world is **AIDS.** It is a disease of the immune system, which becomes deficient and cannot work properly. AIDS is caused by a virus known as **HIV.** This can be spread by sexual contact with someone who has HIV, or by using drug equipment such as needles and syringes already used by someone with HIV/AIDS. It can also be passed from a mother with HIV to her baby in the womb.

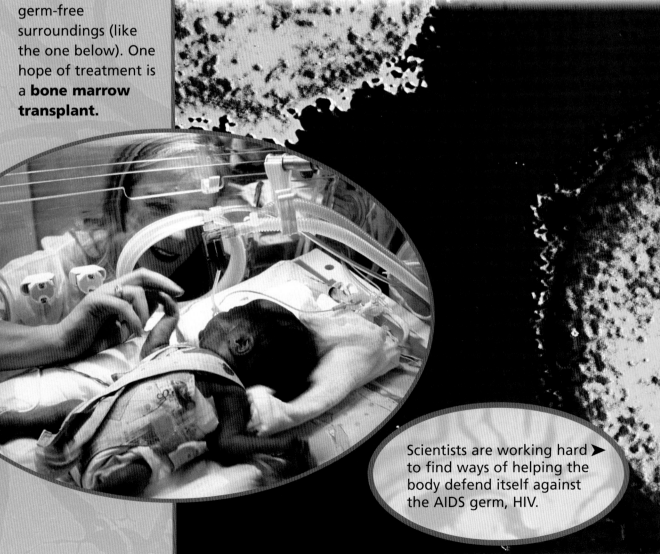

Scientists are working hard ➤ to find ways of helping the body defend itself against the AIDS germ, HIV.

AIDS   Aquired Immune Deficiency Syndrome, caused by HIV
HIV   Human Immunodeficiency Virus. It affects the immune system and causes AIDS.

Attacking the defenders

HIV attacks the body's defenses. In particular it targets the types of **lymphocytes** called T4 cells, which are an essential part of the immune system. Without them, the immune defenses break down. Germs can multiply more easily. People with AIDS begin to suffer from infections such as tuberculosis and pneumonia. Medical drugs can slow down the development of AIDS greatly. At present there is no **vaccine** to prevent infection and no cure.

Turn it down

It may be useful to tone down the body's immune system so it isn't as strong, using **immunosuppressive** drugs. This is done when someone receives a transplant such as a heart, liver, or kidney. Otherwise the body would defend itself by rejecting this strange new object inside it.

A PERSONAL FIGHT

In some people the immune system defends not against germs, or even harmless items like pollen, but against the body itself. Such problems are called autoimmune disorders. They include certain forms of diabetes, psoriasis, and multiple sclerosis.

autoimmune disorder disease in which the body's immune system attacks its own tissues

Stay Out of Danger

Your body has an amazing set of defenses, including your outer skin, mucus linings in your airways, acid in your stomach, blood that clots, and the germ-killing **immune system** deep inside. But you can also defend yourself by thinking and making smart choices. By thinking about what you do beforehand, you can defend yourself in advance. In this way you can take better care of your body.

No worries!

Every day we do dozens of things that hardly seem dangerous at all, like crossing the street (like the couple below) or even chewing our food. We've done it so many times, we don't pay attention. But these familiar actions are sometimes when people get hurt or even killed. Defending yourself requires constant care and awareness.

Safer danger

You probably get tempted sometimes to take dares or small risks. In fact nearly everything we do carries some risk. Avoiding all danger is boring. Risks can be exciting, give us a buzz, and make life interesting. However, there are ways of making risks safer.

Whether it is playing a sport, making new friends, visiting an unknown place, or learning a new skill like rock climbing, we can plan ahead to reduce the dangers. For example, we can read maps or wear the right clothing when we go exploring. By taking responsibility for your own body in this way you protect yourself, prevent harm, and stay happier and healthier.

Amazing stunts like these ▼ don't come easily. They need plenty of practice and perhaps coaching from an expert, but the results are well worth it.

ACCIDENTS HAPPEN!

Many serious accidents happen in familiar situations when people forget to take proper care.

It is very common for people to have accidents at home, particularly in the kitchen or bathroom.

Enjoy life, but remember to take care of yourself.

Medical help

Doctors and medicines can assist the body's defenses in many ways. **Antibiotic** drugs work against **bacteria** that cause infection. Killing viruses is much more difficult. Scientists are only now beginning to develop **antiviral** drugs that work.

Resist and defend

Your body can only defend itself well if it is strong. Otherwise its defense systems cannot work, making infections and other illnesses more likely. Apart from babies and young children, the responsibility for a healthy, fit body lies mainly with its owner. You need to be aware of what keeps you healthy and what is harmful, and make the best choices you can.

Not so obvious

Sometimes the effects of our choices are not so obvious. Staying up very late often or skipping meals may seem harmless. But it makes the body run down, tired, and lack energy. Gradually its levels of stress go up. The body is so busy with the stress, it is less able to resist germs and illness.

Keep fighting fit if you ➤ want your immune system to defend you.

antibiotic substance that acts against bacteria
antiviral substance that acts against viruses

Also the defenses work better if the body has a varied diet, with lots of fresh fruits and vegetables and not too much salt or fatty animal foods. For example, a poor diet can make the skin thinner and more brittle. Then it is more likely to split open when injured and let in germs.

Self defense

Your body defenses might seem complicated and separate from the outside world. They involve chemical substances and billions of **microscopic** cells deep within us. But the risks and dangers you need protection from are affected by what you do, think, say, eat and choose. It's up to you.

Destroying defenses

Everyone knows that smoking tobacco does great damage to the body. One of its effects is to kill the tiny **cilia** hairs that sweep dust and germs out of the lungs. Yet people still smoke. Is each cigarette really worth all the harm it does?

Find Out More

Books

Ballard, Carol. *The Immune System: Injury, Illness and Health*. Chicago: Heinemann Library, 2003

Derkins, Susan. *The Immune System*. New York: Rosen Publishing Group, 2001

Gedatus, Gustave Mark. *HIV and AIDS*. Minneapolis, MN: Compass Point Books, 2000

Winston, Robert. *Body: An Amazing Tour of Human Anatomy*. New York: Dorling Kindersley, 2005

Townsend, John. *Pox, Pus and Plagues: A History of Disease and Infection*. Chicago: Raintree, 2005

World Wide Web

If you want to find out more about the immune system, you can search the Internet using keywords like these:

- "immune system"
- asthma + dust
- hay fever
- AIDS
- vaccination

You can also find your own keywords by using headings or words from this book. Use the search tips on the opposite page to help you find the most useful Web sites.

Place to visit

For loads of information about microbes, disease, and defending yourself, visit:

American Museum of Natural History, Central Park West on 79th Street, New York City, NY 10024-5192

Tel: (212) 769-5100

Or visit the museum web site:

www.amnh.org/ nationalcenter/ infection

Search tips

There are billions of pages on the Internet. It can be difficult to find exactly what you are looking for. These tips will help you find useful Web sites more quickly:

- Know what you want to find out about.
- Use two to six keywords in a search, putting the most important words first.
- Be precise—and only use names of people, places, or things
- If you want to find words that go together, put quote marks around them, for example, "stomach acid" or "length of intestine."
- Use the advanced section of your search engine
- Use the + sign between keywords to link them.

Where to search

Search engine
A search engine looks through millions of Web site pages. It lists all the sites that match the words in the search box. It can give thousands of links, but you will find the best matches are at the top of the list, on the first page. Try **google.com**

Search directory
A search directory is like a library of Web sites that have been sorted by a person instead of a computer. You can search by keyword or subject and browse through the different sites like you look through books on a library shelf. A good example is **yahooligans.com**

Glossary

adenoidectomy operation to remove adenoids

adenoids tissue in the nasal chamber that is part of the lymphatic system

AIDS Aquired Immune Deficiency Syndrome, caused by HIV

allergic reaction processes such as inflammation or coughing as the body fights a substance that is harmless to most people

allergy sensitivity to a substance that is normally harmless, like pollen

antibiotic substance that acts against bacteria

antibodies substances made by the immune system that attack antigens

antigens substances that are not part of the body and are recognized and attacked by the immune system

antiviral substance that acts against viruses

asthma condition, often linked to allergy, where the bronchioles get narrow and fill with mucus, making breathing difficult

autoimmune disorder disease in which the body's immune system attacks its own tissues

bacteria microscopic organisms of many types

B-cell type of white blood cell that makes antibodies to attack antigens

blood vessels arteries, capillaries, and veins through which blood flows

calluses patches of thick, hardened skin

cancer disease caused when body cells multiply out of control and spread, causing growths or lumps called malignant tumors

capillaries tiniest blood vessles with very thin walls

cells microscopic building blocks that make up all body parts

cilia microscopic hairlike projections on the cells in various body parts

clot lump of blood that seals a wound

contagious spread by close contact

dermis inner layer of skin containing sweat glands, hair roots, and nerve sensors

digest break down food into smaller and smaller pieces

digestive juices liquids in the digestive system that break food apart

donor person who gives something

ducts pipes or tubes for liquid

enzyme substance that controls the speed of a chemical change, such as occurs during digestion

epidermis outer layer of skin, constantly renewed from underneath

HIV Human Immunodeficiency Virus. It affects the immune system and causes AIDS.

immune system cells and body structures that protect the body from illness

immune resistant to a certain infection and able to destroy the germs before they multiply and cause illness

immunization the process of becoming resistant, or immune, to a certain illness

immunosuppressive tones down the body's immune system to make it less sensitive

incubation period the time between germs getting into the body and when the effects or symptoms of illness begin

inflammation body's response to damage, germs or disease. Fluids collect and white blood cells gather causing redness, swelling, pain, and heat.

keratin tough protein that makes skin resistant to wear

lymph nodes masses of tissue that act as filters to collect harmful germs and contain white blood cells to fight the germs

lymph pale fluid that flows through vessels and ducts and transports white blood cells

lymphocytes types of white blood cells that fight germs

macrophage white blood cell that eats bacteria and other unwanted germs

microscopic something so small that it can only be seen under a microscope

mucus sticky fluid in various body parts, that gathers pieces of dust and germs, so they can be moved out of the body

parasitic living with, in, or on an organism, causing harm to the organism

phlegm sticky fluid in the airways

platelets pieces of cells that take part in clotting

pollen tiny dustlike particles or grains released by plant flowers

protists one-celled organisms

red blood cells cells in the blood speccialized to carry oxygen around the body

reflexes automatic reactions like blinking or coughing

resistant protected against or able to fight an illness

sebum oily substance made by skin to protect itself and stay flexible

thymus gland near the heart that is part of the lymphatic system

tonsillectomy operation to remove tonsils

tonsils masses of tissue inside the throat that are part of the lymphatic system

toxin harmful or poisonous substance

transplant when a body part is replaced by one from another body

vaccination putting modified germs into the body to make it immune to a certain disease

vaccine substance containing modified versions of a germ, which prepares the immune system to defend against the real germs

viruses tiniest germs that can cause serious diseases

white blood cells colorless cells in the blood that fight germs and disease

Index

Body language   adrenaline   (definition to come)
senses   (defintion to come)